WILTSHIRE
Wit & Humour

CHANTELLE LYDIARD

BRADWELL
BOOKS

Published by Bradwell Books
9 Orgreave Close Sheffield S13 9NP
Email: books@bradwellbooks.co.uk
Compiled by Chantelle Lydiard

British Library Cataloguing in Publication Data: a catalogue record for this book is available from the British Library.

1st Edition

ISBN: 9781909914568

Print: Gomer Press, Llandysul, Ceredigion SA44 4JL
Design by: jenksdesign@yahoo.co.uk/07506 471162
Illustrations: ©Tim O'Brien 2014

At a primary school in Wootton Rivers, the teacher came up with a good problem for her maths class to solve.

"Suppose, there were a dozen sheep and six of them jumped over a fence," she said to the group of seven-year-olds, "How many would be left?"

Little Harry, a farmer's son, put his hand up. "None," he answered.

"None?" exclaimed his teacher. "Harry, I'm afraid you don't know your arithmetic."

"Really, Miss?" said Harry, cockily, "And you don't know your sheep. When one goes, they all go!"

A gang of robbers broke into the Salisbury Lawyers' Club by mistake. The old legal lions put up a fierce fight for their lives and their money. The gang was happy to escape in one piece.

"It ain't so bad," one crook said. "At least we got fifty quid between us."

His boss screamed at him, "I warned you to stay clear of lawyers... we had 200 quid when we broke in!"

At The Blue Boar in Aldbourne, a newcomer asked an elderly local regular, "Have you lived here all your life?" The old man took a sip of his ale and, after a long pause, replied, "Don't know yet!"

At a cricket match in Beanacre, a fast bowler sent one down and it just clipped the bail. As nobody yelled "Ow's att", the batsman picked up the bail and replaced it. He looked at the umpire and said, "Windy today isn't it?"

"Yes," said the umpire, "Mind it doesn't blow your cap off when you're walking back to the pavilion."

A Wiltshire man is driving through Hampshire, when he passes a farmer standing in the middle of a huge field. He pulls the car over and watches the farmer standing stock-still, doing absolutely nothing. Intrigued, the man walks over to the farmer and asks him, "Excuse me sir, but what are you doing?"

The farmer replies, "I'm trying to win a Nobel Prize."

"How?" Asks the puzzled Wiltshire man.

"Well," says the farmer, "I heard they give the prize to people who are outstanding in their field."

My wife had a nice pub lunch in a Wiltshire market town

Chippenham?

No, it was a cheese ploughman's

Why couldn't the lifeguard save the hippie?

He was too far out, man!

A harried man runs into his GP's surgery.

"Doctor! Doctor! My wife's in labour! But she keeps screaming, 'Shouldn't, couldn't, wouldn't, can't!'"

"Oh, that's okay," says the doctor. "She's just having contractions."

One day a Hampshire boy was in the back garden shouting,

"Mum, why is my Portsmouth F.C. top lying on the grass?"

His Mum looked out the window and shouted,

"The thieving gits stole my pegs!"

A passenger in a taxi tapped the driver on the shoulder to ask him something.

The driver screamed, lost control of the cab, nearly hit a bus, drove up over the curb and stopped just inches from a large plate glass window.

For a few moments everything was silent in the cab, then the driver said, "Please, don't ever do that again. You scared the daylights out of me."

The passenger, who was also frightened, apologised and said he didn't realise that a tap on the shoulder could frighten him so much, to which the driver replied, "I'm sorry, it's really not your fault at all. Today is my first day driving a cab. I've been driving a hearse for the last twenty-five years."

A group of backpackers from Wiltshire College were sitting around a campfire one evening when a stranger asked to join them. Glad to add to their group, they agreed. The evening's fun soon turned to jokes. One of the students started to tell jokes in which Southampton Uni was the butt of the humour. The stranger who, it turned out, had graduated from Southampton University himself, became more and more furious with each quip. Finally, he had had enough and pulled out his razor and began to threaten the Wiltshire lads with it. Fortunately for them, he couldn't find a socket to plug it into.

I had a car accident with a magician – he came out of nowhere

Supporters, waiting to watch Swindon Town play Portsmouth, heard that the Pompey players were going to be delayed.

They saw a sign on the motorway that said "Clean Lavatories"... so they did.

A plain Jane from Box goes to see Madame Grizelda, an Avebury fortune-teller, and asks about her future love life.

Madame Grizelda tells her, "Two men are madly in love with you – Mark and Maurice."

"Who will be the lucky one?" asks Jane excitedly.

Madame Grizelda answers, "Maurice will marry you, and Mark will be the lucky one."

"You're looking glum, "the captain of Spye Park C.C. remarked to one of his players.

"Yes, the doctor says I can't play cricket," said the downcast man.

"Really?" replied the captain, "I didn't know he'd ever seen you play?"

A man went to the doctor one day and said, "I've just been playing rugby for Devizes and when I got back, I found that when I touched my legs, my arms, my head, and everywhere else, it really hurt."

After a careful examination the doctor concluded, "you have a broken finger."

A man from Royal Wootton Bassett decided to become a monk so he went to the monastery and talked to the head monk.

The head monk said, "You must take a vow of silence and can only say two words every three years."

The man agreed and after the first three years, the head monk came to him and said, "What are your two words?"

"Food cold!" the man replied.

Three more years went by and the head monk came to him and said, "What are your two words?"

"Robe dirty!" the man exclaimed.

Three more years went by and the head monk came to him and said, "What are your two words?"

"I quit!" said the man.

"Well," the head monk replied, "I'm not surprised. You've done nothing but complain ever since you got here!"

There's a man in Andover who claims to have invented a game that's a bit like cricket; what he doesn't realise is Hampshire County Cricket Club's been playing it for years.

A Melksham man fell out with his in-laws and banned them from entering the house while he was in it. His wife faithfully carried out his wishes until she was on her death bed and then asked sadly, "Haven't I always been a supportive wife to you, John?"

"Yes, my dear," he replied, "The best."

"Then I would love it if you could grant my last request and let my sister Sarah ride in the first car with you at my funeral?"

"Alright, my dear," he agreed heavily, "But I'm warning you, it'll spoil all my pleasure!"

Two blokes are standing in the Chippenham Job Centre, waiting for their turn at the counter.

The first bloke says to the second one, "I have to buy my wife something nice for our wedding anniversary and the benefits cheque won't cover it."

The second bloke looks up from his paper and says, "What date?"

The first bloke thinks for a while and says, "15th September."

The second bloke considers his next question. "What year?"

Without taking a breath, the first bloke replies, "Every year for the last twenty-seven!"

Two council workers on a site in Salisbury are surveying land they're about to dig up.

The gaffer says to one of them, " You go and get the metal detector and check for pipe work and I'll get the kettle on and have a brew."

The gaffer gets the tea going while his mate starts work. Half an hour later the gaffer puts his paper down, next to his mug of tea, to find out how work is progressing and he finds his mate sitting on a wall scratching his head.

"What's up with you?" The gaffer asks. "There's pipework all over the place. Look!"

The young worker sets off across the land, the bleeper

sounding continuously as the detector passes in front of him.

The gaffer watches him, laughing, then he says, "Are you soft or what? You've got steel toe caps in your boots!"

Down the King's Head, a group of blokes sit around drinking when a mobile phone on the table rings. One of the men picks up the mobile and puts the speaker-phone on.

A woman's voice says, "How are you, darling? I hope you don't mind but I've just seen a diamond ring priced £2000 and wondered if I can buy it? I've got your credit card with me."

"Of course, my dear, go ahead," answers the man.

"While I'm on," purrs the lady, "I've noticed a top of the range car I'd like. It's only £65,000, could I order that as well?"

"Of course, my angel," replies the man.

His friends around the table look at each other in disbelief as the lady continues, "And I've just noticed a house on the coast, lover. It's only £750,000 - could we have that as well please?"

"Of course, sugar," answers the man, without so much as blinking.

The phone call is ended and the man smiles at the others and takes a long swill of beer. Then he looks around and shouts "Anyone know whose phone this is?"

It was match day for the 'Robins' and excited crowds filled the streets of Swindon, heading for the stadium. A funeral procession drove slowly through the throng. One of the Swindon Town supporters stopped, took off his hat and bowed reverently as the hearse passed.

"That was a nice thing to do," remarked his mate.

"Well," said the 'Robins' fan, "She was a good wife to me for thirty odd years."

Pupil: "I don't think I deserved zero on this test!"

Teacher: "I agree, but that's the lowest mark I could give you!"

Derek and Duncan were long-time neighbours in Wroughton. Every time, Derek saw Duncan coming round to his house, his heart sank. This was because he knew that, as always, Duncan would be visiting him in order to borrow something and he was fed up with it.

"I'm not going to let Duncan get away with it this time," he said quietly to his wife, "Watch what I'm about to do."

"Hi there, I wondered if you were thinking about using your hedge trimmer this afternoon?" asked Duncan.

"Oh, I'm very sorry," said Derek, trying to look apologetic, "but I'm actually going to be using it all afternoon."

"In that case," replied Duncan with a big grin, "You won't be using your golf clubs, will you? Mind if I borrow them?"

Two Beehive Cricket Club players are chatting in the bar after a match. "So did you have a hard time explaining last week's game to the wife?" says one.

"I certainly did," says the other, "She found out I wasn't there!"

Psychiatrist: "What's your problem?"

Patient: "I think I'm a chicken."

Psychiatrist: "How long has this been going on?"

Patient: "Ever since I was an egg!"

Teacher: "Why have you got cotton wool in your ears, do you have an infection?"

Pupil: "Well, sir, you keep saying that things go in one ear and out the other so I am trying to keep them all in."

Three Wiltshire women are talking in a bar about a party they've been invited to.

The first one says, "We've got to all wear an item that matches something belonging to our husbands at this party, haven't we?"

"Yeah," said the other two, "But what?"

The first one continued, "Well, my husband's got black hair and I've got a little black dress I can diet into by then."

The second one says, "That's a good idea. My husband has got brown hair and I've got a brown dress I can diet into by then too."

The third one looks a bit hesitant and says, "I just need to go on a diet - my husband's bald!"

"Dad," says the little boy," Can I play football with the lads in the street?"

"No, "says his dad, "They swear too much."

"But you play with them, Dad?"

"I swear already."

A lad from Crudwell who had just started his first term at Winchester University asked a third year, "Can you tell me where the library's at?"

The older student said disdainfully, "At Winchester University, we never end a sentence with a preposition." The new boy tried again, "Can you tell me where the library's at, you wally?"

Darren proudly drove his new convertible into Chippenham and parked it on the main street. He was on his way to the recycling centre to get rid of an unwanted gift, a foot spa, which he left on the back seat.

He had walked half way down the street when he realised that he had left the top down with the foot spa still in the back.

He ran all the way back to his car, but it was too late...another five foot spas had been dumped in the car.

Question: Why did the Mushroom get invited to all the parties?

Answer: 'Coz he's a fungi!

Question: How do you make gold soup?

Answer: Put 24 carrots in it.

Swindon Town beat Portsmouth five – nothing; they were lucky to get nothing.

Ten women out on a hen night in Swindon thought it would be sensible if one of them stayed more sober than the other nine and looked after the money to pay for their drinks. After deciding who would hold the money, they all put twenty pounds into the kitty to cover expenses. At closing time after a few beers, several vodka and cokes, and a Pina Colada each, they stood around deciding how to divvy up the leftover cash.

"How do we stand?" said Sharon.

"Stand?!" said Debbie. "That's the easy part! I'm wondering how I can walk. I've missed the last bus to Cricklade!"

A lawyer at Wiltshire Crown Court says to the judge, "Your Honour, I wish to appeal my client's case on the basis of newly discovered evidence."

His Lordship replies, "And what is the nature of the new evidence?"

The lawyer says, "My Lord, I discovered that my client still has £500 left."

Did you hear about the magic tractor? It drove up the lane and turned into a field.

A man rushed into Great Western Hospital and asked a nurse for a cure for hiccups. Grabbing a cup of water, the nurse quickly splashed it into the man's face.

"What did you that for?" screamed the man, wiping his face.

"Well, you don't have the hiccups now, do you?" said the nurse.

"No," replied the man. "But my wife out in the car does."

At an antiques auction in Castle Combe, a wealthy American announced that he had lost his wallet containing £5,000, and he would give a reward of £50 to the person who found it.

From the back of the hall a local man shouted, "I'll give £100!"

One afternoon at Winchester University, a group of freshers, who had just started their psychology course, were attending one of their first seminars. The topic was emotional extremes.

"Let's begin by discussing some contrasts," said the tutor. He pointed to a student in the front row, "What is the opposite of joy?"

The student thought about it briefly, then answered "Sadness."

The tutor asked another student, "What is the opposite of depression?"

She paused then said, "Elation."

"And you," the tutor said to another student sitting at the back, "What about the opposite of woe?"

The student thought for a moment, then replied, "Um, I believe that would be 'giddy up'."

One Sunday in St Mary's church, Steeple Ashton, the vicar opened his Bible and began to read the lesson. In a loud voice, he proclaimed, "Corinthians 7."

A keen Swindon Town fan, who had been dozing in the front pew, woke up with a start and shouted out, "Blimey! Who were they playing?"

One winter's night, a lorry is going along the road near Ludgershall when the car behind, driving in from Hampshire, starts flashing its headlights and sounding its horn. This goes on for a good ten minutes before the car finally overtakes the lorry on the dual carriageway and as it does so the driver, who is from Andover, rolls the window down and shouts to the lorry driver, "Hey, you! Don't you realise you're losing your load off the back?"

"I blooming well hope so!" The lorry driver shouts back. "I'm gritting the roads, ain't I!?"

In a school in Upavon, a little boy just wasn't getting good marks. One day, his teacher was checking his homework and said, "Lee, once again I'm afraid I can only give you two out of ten."

Little Lee looked up at her and said, "Well, Miss, I don't want to scare you, but…"

He stopped, a worried expression on his face.

"What is it? Tell me, Lee," said his teacher kindly.

"Well," said the boy, "my daddy says if I don't get better marks soon, somebody is going to get a spanking."

A couple from the Kington Langley had been courting for nearly twenty years. One day as they sat on a seat in the park, the woman plucked up the courage to ask,

"Don't you think it's time we got married?"

Her sweetheart answered,

"Yes, but who'd have us?"

Four Southampton University students taking their chemistry degree had done very well in their exams so far. Because of this, even though their last exam of the year was fast approaching, the four friends decided to go back to their hometown and catch up with some friends there. They had a great time partying.

However, after all the fun, they slept all day on Sunday and didn't make it back to Southampton until early Monday morning which was the time of their final exam. Rather than taking the exam, they decided to find their professor after it was over and explain to him why they missed it. They told him that they had gone home to do some studying for the weekend and had planned to come back in time for the exam. But unfortunately, they had a flat tyre on the way back, didn't have a spare, and couldn't get help for a long time. As a result, they had only just arrived!

The professor thought it over and then agreed they could make up their final exam the following day. The four were very relieved. They studied hard that night - all night - and went in the next day at the time the professor had told them. He placed them in separate rooms and handed each of them a test booklet and told them to begin.

The first problem was worth five points. It was something simple about a specific chemistry topic. "Great," they all thought, "This is going to be easy." They each finished the problem and turned the page. On the second page was written, "Question 2 (for 95 points): Which tyre?"

An old bloke at the bus stop outside Great Western Hospital is talking to the next person in the queue whilst rubbing his head.

"My wooden leg ain't half giving me some gyp," complained the old boy.

The person in the queue looks at him, wondering why he keeps rubbing his head, and says, "Really? Why?"

The old man retorted, "Cos my missus keeps hitting me over the head with it!"

The president of the Chippenham Vegetarian Society really couldn't control himself any more. He simply had to try some pork, just to see what it tasted like. So one day he told his members he was going away for a short break. He left town and headed to a restaurant in Corsham. He sat down, ordered a roasted pig, and waited impatiently for his treat. After only a few minutes, he heard someone call his name, and, to his horror, he saw one of his members walking towards him. At exactly the same moment, the waiter arrived at his table, with a huge platter, holding a whole roasted pig with an apple in its mouth. "Isn't this place something?" said the president, thinking quickly, "Look at the way they serve apples!"

Sam worked in a telephone marketing company in Devizes. One day he walked into his boss's office and said, "I'll be honest with you, I know the economy isn't great, but I have three companies after me, and, with respect, I would like to ask for a pay rise."

After a few minutes of haggling, his manager finally agreed to a 5% pay rise, and Sam happily got up to leave.

"By the way," asked the boss as Sam went to the door, "Which three companies are after you?"

"The electric company, the water company, and the phone company," Sam replied.

A farmer was driving along a country road near the village of Lacock with a large load of fertiliser. A little boy, playing in front of his house, saw him and called out, "What do you have on your truck?"

"Fertiliser," the farmer replied.

"What are you going to do with it?" asked the little boy. "Put it on strawberries," answered the farmer. "You ought to live here," the little boy advised him. "We put sugar and cream on ours."

It was a quiet night in Sutton Veny and a man and his wife were fast asleep, when there was an unexpected knock on the door. The man looked at his alarm clock. It was half past three in the morning. "I'm not getting out of bed at this time," he thought and rolled over.

There was another louder knock.

"Aren't you going to answer that?" asked his wife irritably.

So the man dragged himself out of bed and went downstairs. He opened the door to find a strange man standing outside. It didn't take the homeowner long to realise the man was drunk. "Hi there," slurred the stranger. "Can you give me a push?" "No, I'm sorry I most certainly can't. It's half past three in the morning and I was in bed," said the man and he slammed the front door.

He went back up to bed and told his wife what happened. "That wasn't very nice of you," she said. "Remember that night we broke down in the pouring rain on the way to pick the kids up from the babysitter, and you had to knock on that man's door to get us started again? What would have happened if he'd told us to get lost?"

"But the man who just knocked on our door was drunk," replied her husband.

"Well, we can at least help move his car somewhere safe and sort him out a taxi," said his wife. "He needs our help."

So the husband got out of bed again, got dressed, and went downstairs. He opened the door, but couldn't to see the stranger anywhere so he shouted, "Hey, do you still want a push?"

In answer, he heard a voice call out, "Yes please!"

So, still unable to see the stranger, he shouted, "Where are you?" "I'm over here, mate," the stranger replied, "on your swing."

Patient: "Doctor, doctor! I keep thinking I'm a dog."

Doctor: "Please, take a seat."

Patient: "I'm not allowed on the furniture."

Phil's nephew came to him with a problem. "I have my choice of two women," he said, with a worried frown, "A beautiful, penniless young girl whom I love dearly, and a rich widow who I don't really love."

"Follow your heart," Phil counselled, "marry the girl you love."

"Very well, Uncle Phil," said the nephew, "That's sound advice. Thank you."

"You're welcome," replied Phil with a smile, "By the way, where does the widow live?"

A high-rise building was going up in Swindon, and three steel erectors sat on a girder having their lunch.

"Oh, no, not cheese and pickle again," said Jim, the first one, "If I get the same again tomorrow, I'll jump off the girder.'

Horace opened his packet. "Oh, no, not a chicken salad with lettuce and mayo," he said. "If I get the same again tomorrow, I'll jump off too."

Andy, the third man, opened his lunch. "Oh, no, not another potato sandwich," he said. "If I get the same again tomorrow, I'll follow you two off the girder."

The next day, Jim got cheese and pickle. Without delay, he jumped. Horace saw he had chicken salad with lettuce and mayo, and, with a wild cry, he leapt too. Then the third man, Andy, opened his lunchbox. "Oh, no," he said. "Potato sandwiches." And he too jumped.

The foreman, who had overheard their conversation, reported what had happened, and the funerals were held together.

"If only I'd known," sobbed Jim's wife.

"If only he'd said," wailed Horace's wife.

"I don't understand it at all," said Andy's wife. "He always got his own sandwiches ready."

A farmer from Petersfield once visited a farmer based near Warminster. The visitor asked, "How big is your farm?" to which the Wiltshire farmer replied, "Can you see those trees over there? That's the boundary of my farmland".

"Is that all?" said the Hampshire farmer, "It takes me three days to drive to the boundary of my farm."

The Warminster man looked at him and said, "I had a car like that once."

The nervous young batsman playing for Buscott Park C.C. was having a very bad day. In a quiet moment in the game, he muttered to the one of his team mates, "Well, I suppose you've seen worse players."

There was no response...so he said it again, "I said 'I guess you've seen worse players'."

His team mate looked at him and answered, "I heard you the first time. I was just trying to think..."

One day at Savernake Hospital, a group of primary school children were being given a tour. A nurse showed them the x-ray machines and asked them if they had ever had broke a bone.

One little boy raised his hand, "I did!"

"Did it hurt?" the nurse asked.

"No!" he replied.

"Wow, you must be a very brave boy!" said the nurse. "What did you break?"

"My sister's arm!"

A woman from Malmesbury called Mandy was still not married at thirty-five and she was getting really tired of going to family weddings especially because her old Aunt Maud always came over and said, "You're next!"

It made Mandy so annoyed she racked her brains to figure out how to get Aunt Maud to stop. Sadly, an old uncle died and there was a big family funeral. Mandy spotted Aunt Maud in the crematorium, walked over, pointed at the coffin and said, with a big smile, "You're next!"

Two elderly ladies were enjoying a small sherry in their local in Brokenborough.

One said to the other, "Was it love at first sight when you met your late husband?"

"No, I don't think so," came the reply, "I didn't know how much money he had when I first met him!"

An elderly couple from Dorcan are sitting at the dining table in their semi-detached house talking about making preparations for writing their wills. Bill says to his missus, Edna, "I've been thinking, my dear, if I go first to meet me maker I don't want you to be on your own for too long. In fact, I think you could do worse than marry Colin in the Chemists or Dave with the fruit stall in the market. They'd provide for you and look after you when I'm gone."

"That's very kind on you to think about me like that, Bill," replied Edna, "But I've already made my own arrangements!"

At a school in Didmarton, the maths teacher poses a question to little Josh, "If I give £500 to your dad on 12% interest per annum, what will I get back after two years."

 "Nothing," says Josh.

"I am afraid you know nothing about maths, Josh," says the teacher crossly.

"I am afraid too, sir," replies Josh, "You know nothing about my father."

An expectant father rang the Trowbridge Maternity Unit to see how his wife, who had gone into labour, was getting on. By mistake, he was connected to the Wiltshire County Cricket ground.

"How's it going?" he asked.

"Fine," came the answer, "We've got three out and hope to have the rest out before lunch. The last one was a duck."

Patient: "Doctor, doctor! I've broken my arm in a couple of places!"

Doctor: "Then stay away from those places!"

Did you hear about the last wish of the henpecked husband of a house-proud wife?

He asked to have his ashes scattered on the carpet.

Did you hear about the truck driver from Southampton who was seen desperately chiselling away at the brickwork after his lorry became stuck at the entrance to a tunnel?

"Why don't you let some air out of your tyres?" asked a helpful passer-by.

"No, mate," replied the driver, "It's the roof that won't go under, not the wheels."

BEWARE LOW BRIDGE!

A police officer arrived at the scene of a major pile up on the M4.

The officer runs over to the front car and asks the driver, "Are you seriously hurt?"

The driver turns to the officer and says, "How the heck should I know? Do I look like a lawyer?"

A pupil at a school in Pewsey asked his teacher, "Are 'trousers' singular or plural?"

The teacher replied, "They're singular on top and plural on the bottom."

Pete and Larry hadn't seen each other in many years. They were having a long chat, telling each other all about their lives. Finally Pete invited Larry to visit him in his new flat in Trowbridge. "I have a wife and three kids and I'd love to have you visit us."

"Great. Where do you live?"

"Here's the address. There's plenty of parking behind the flat. Park and come around to the front door, kick it open with your foot, go to the lift and press the button with your left elbow, then enter! When you reach the sixth floor, go down the hall until you see my name on the door. Then press the doorbell with your right elbow and I'll let you in."

"Great. But tell me...what is all this business of kicking the front door open, then pressing elevator buttons with my right, then my left elbow?

Pete answered, "Surely you're not coming empty-handed?"

A police officer was patrolling the lanes outside Salisbury one night, when he noticed a car swerving all over the road. Quickly, he turned on his lights and siren and pulled the driver over. "Sir, do you know you're all over the road? Please step out of the car."

When the man got out of the car, the policeman told him to walk in a straight line.

"I'd be happy to, offisher," said the drunk, "If you can just get the line to stop moving about."

Three blondes were walking near the Savernake Forest when they came upon a set of tracks.

The first blonde said, "Those are deer tracks."

The second blonde said, "No, those are horse tracks."

The third blonde said, "You're both wrong, those are cattle tracks."

The Blondes were still arguing when the 11.20 to Marlborough hit them.

Anne and Matt, a couple from Broad Hinton, went to the Wiltshire County Show at Marlborough and found a weighing scale that tells your fortune and weight.

"Hey, listen to this," said Matt, showing his wife a small white card. "It says I'm bright, energetic, and a great husband."

"Yeah," Anna said, "And it has your weight wrong too."

A policeman stops a drunk wandering the streets of Swindon at four in the morning and says, "Can you explain why you are out at this hour, sir?"

The drunk replies, "If I was able to explain myself, I would have been home with the wife ages ago."

A new dentist set up a surgery in Upper Upham and quickly acquired a reputation for being a "Painless" dentist. But soon a local chap disputed this.

"He's a fake!" he told his mates. "He's not painless at all. When he stuck his finger in my mouth I bit him - and he yelled like anyone else."

What do you get if you cross the Swindon Town with an OXO cube?

A laughing stock.

When the manager of Southampton started to tell the team about tactics, half the players thought he was talking about a new kind of peppermint.

An old chap from Urchfont went to the G.P.

"Doctor," says the old boy, "I feels a bit loppity, you know - a bit under the weather."

"Flu?" asks the doc.

"No," says the old chap, "I rode here on my bike like I always does."

A Hurrah Henry from Hampshire was driving around Salisbury in his fancy new car and realised that he was lost. The driver stopped a local character, old Tom, and said, "Hey, you there! Old man, what happens if I turn left here?"

"Don't know sir," replied Tom.

"Well, what if I turn right here - where will that take me?" continued the visitor.

"Don't know, sir," replied old Tom.

Becoming exasperated, the driver continued, "Well, what if I go straight on?"

A flicker of knowledge passed over old Tom's face but then he replied, "Don't know, sir."

"I say old man you don't know a lot do you?" retorted the posh bloke.

Old Tom looked at him and said, "I may not know a lot, sir, but I ain't lost like what you are!" With that, old Tom walked off leaving the motorist stranded.

An elderly husband and wife from Goatacre visit their doctor when they begin forgetting little things. Their doctor tells them that many people find it useful to write themselves little notes.

When they get home, the wife says, "Dear, will you please go to the kitchen and get me a dish of ice cream? And maybe write that down so you won't forget?"

"Nonsense," says the husband, "I can remember a dish of ice cream."

"Well," says the wife, "I'd also like some strawberries and whipped cream on it."

"My memory's not all that bad," says the husband. "No problem - a dish of ice cream with strawberries and whipped cream. I don't need to write it down."

He goes into the kitchen; his wife hears pots and pans banging around. The husband finally emerges from the kitchen and presents his wife with a plate of bacon and eggs. She looks at the plate and asks, "Hey, where's the toast I asked for?

For a minute Portsmouth were in with a chance – then the game started.

A labourer in Mildenhall, shouted up to his roofer mate on top of an old terraced house, saying, "Don't start climbing down this ladder, Bert."

"Why not?" Bert called back.

"Cos I moved it five minutes ago!" replied his mate.

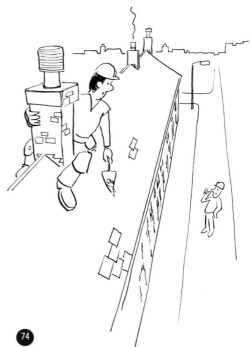

A reporter from The Wiltshire Times was covering the local football league and went to see Southbrook F.C. versus Shrewton United. One of the Southbrook players looked so old he went over to him and said, "You know you might be the oldest man playing in the league. How do you do it at your age?"

The man replied, "I drink six pints every night, smoke two packets of fags a day, and eat tons of chips."

"Wow, that is incredible!" said the reporter, "How old did you say you were?"

"Twenty-two," said the player proudly.

A bloke walked up to the foreman of a road laying gang in Swindon and asked for a job. "I haven't got one for you today," said the foreman, looking up from his newspaper. "But if you walk half a mile down there, you'll find the gang and you can see if you like the work. I can put you on the list for tomorrow."

"That's great, mate," said the bloke as he wandered off down the road.

At the end of the shift, the man walked past the foreman and shouted, "Thanks, mate. See you in the morning."

The foreman looked up from his paper and called back, "You've enjoyed yourself then?"

"Yes, I have!" the bloke shouted, "But can I have a shovel or a pick to lean on like the rest of the gang tomorrow?"

A Wanborough couple, Enid and Sidney, are having matrimonial difficulties and seek the advice of a counsellor. The couple are shown into a room where the counsellor asks Enid what problems, in her opinion, she faces in her relationship with Sidney.

"Well," she starts, "he shows me no affection, I don't seem to be important to him anymore. We don't share the same interests and I don't think he loves me at all." Enid has tears in her eyes as the counsellor walks over to her, gives her a big hug and kisses her firmly on the lips.

Sidney looks on in passive disbelief. The counsellor turns to Sidney and says, "This is what Enid needs once a day for the next month. Can you see that she gets it?"

Sidney looks unsettled, "Well I can drop her off everyday other than Wednesdays when I play snooker and Sundays when I go fishing!"

A well-known academic from Winchester University was giving a lecture on the philosophy of language at Wiltshire College. He came to a curious aspect of English grammar.

"You will note," said the somewhat stuffy scholar, "That in the English language, two negatives can mean a positive, but it is never the case that two positives can mean a negative."

To which someone at the back responded, "Yeah, yeah."

A DEFRA Inspector goes to a small farm near Trowbridge and knocks on the door of humble, tied cottage. A young boy opens the door and asks what business the man has on his parent's property.

"I've come to inspect the farm for compliance with EU regulations, my boy. Where's your father?"

"You can't speak to him, he's busy," says the surly child.

"I shall speak to him. He's had notice of my visit," the Inspector retorted firmly.

"Well, he's feeding the pigs at the moment, "says the boy, "But you'll be able to tell me father easy enough - he's the one wearing a hat!"